LOOKING AT RELIGIONS

My Sikh Life

Kanwaljit Kaur-Singh

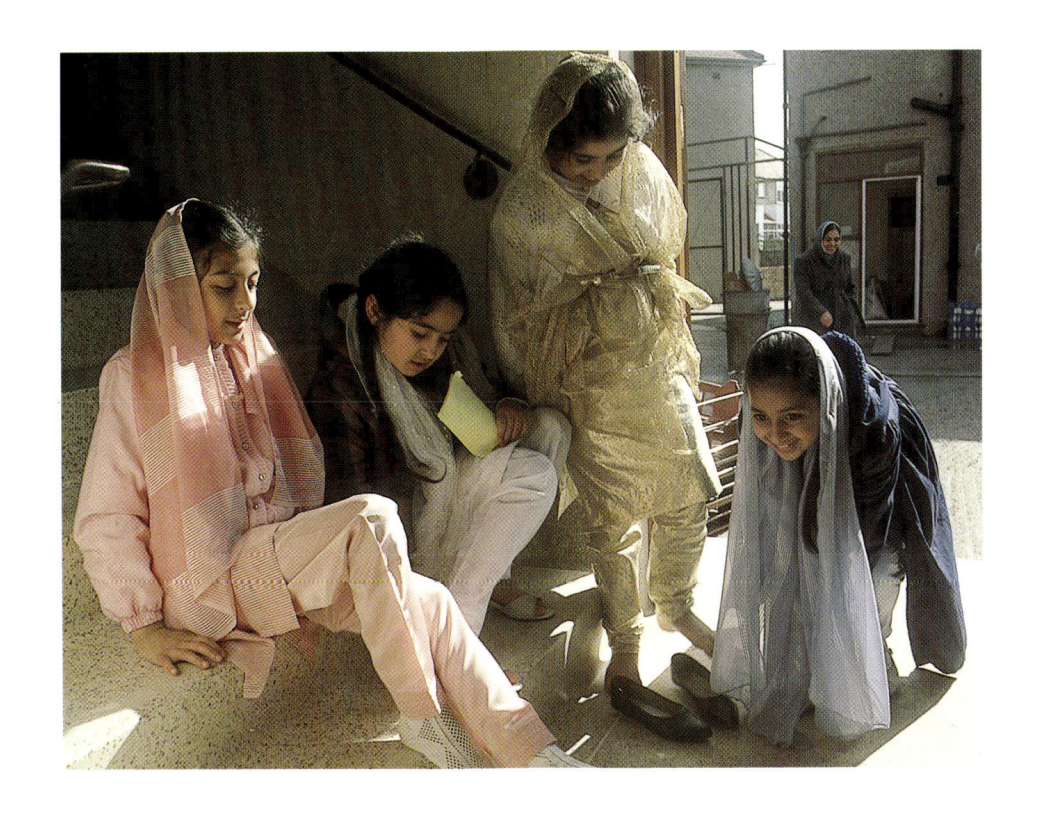

WAYLAND

LOOKING AT RELIGION

My Buddhist Life
My Christian Life
My Hindu Life
My Jewish Life
My Muslim Life
My Sikh Life

Consultant: Alison Seaman
Editor: Ruth Raudsepp
Designer: Joyce Chester

First published in 1997 by Wayland Publishers Ltd under the series title 'Everyday Religion'
This edition published in 2006 by Wayland, an imprint of Hachette Children's Books

Reprinted in 2007

© Copyright 1997 Hodder Wayland

All rights reserved. Apart from any use permitted under UK copyright law, this publication may only be reproduced, stored or transmitted, in any form, or by any means with prior permission in writing of the publishers or in the case of reprographic production in accordance with the terms of licences issued by the Copyright Licensing Agency.

British Library Cataloguing in Publication Data
Kaur-Singh, Kanwaljit
My Sikh Life - (Everyday Religion)
1. Sikhism - Juvenile literature
1. Title
294.6
ISBN-13: 978 0 7502 4957 7

Picture acknowledgements
The publishers would like to thank the following for allowing their pictures to be used in this book: Rupert Horrox *covers*, Impact 11, 13, 15; Christine Osborne *title page*, 8, 14, 16, 18, 19, 20, 21, 22, 26; Ann & Bury Peerless 27; Sikh Educational Advisory Services 10; Kanwaljit kaur-Singh 9, 24, 25; Trip/H Rogers 4, 17; Zak Waters 5, 6, 7, 12, 23. The remaining pictures are from the Wayland Picture Library.

Title page: Sikh children take off their shoes before entering the gurdwara.

Typeset by Joyce Chester
Printed in China

Wayland
338 Euston Road, London NW1 3BH
Wayland is a division of Hachette Children's Books, an Hachette Livre UK Company

Contents

Worship at Home 5

How Sikhs Live 6–11

Worship at the Gurdwara 12–19

Weekend School 20–21

Naming a Sikh Baby 22–23

A Sikh Wedding 24–25

Sikh Festivals 26–27

Notes for Teachers 28–29

Glossary 30

Books to Read 31

Index 32

These children are all Sikhs. There are Sikhs all over the world. It is like being part of one big family.

Randeep Singh and Roopa Kaur are Sikh children. They are listening to the reading of their holy book, the **Guru Granth Sahib**.

Gunraj's uncut hair is tied under a **patka**. Gunraj's father covers his hair with a turban.

Amrit Kaur's mother is plaiting her long uncut hair. She is getting ready to go to school.

Young boys learn to tie their own turbans, usually when they start their secondary school. Here is Harjeet Singh tying his turban.

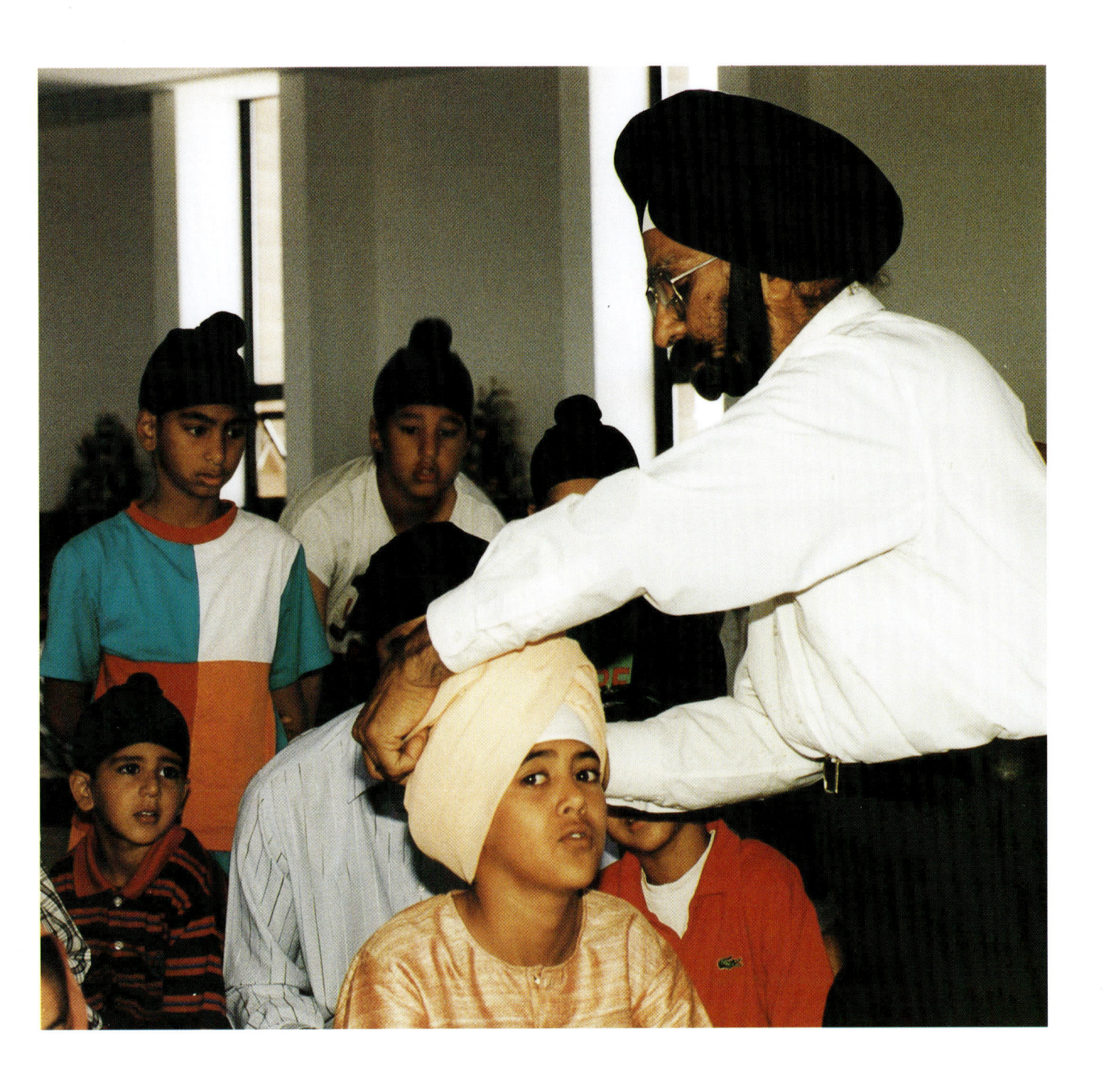

Pavneet Singh's parents held a special service in the **gurdwara** to celebrate the first time he started to tie his turban.

Sikh men are easily recognized by their turbans and uncut beards. Most men wear western clothes such as trousers and jackets.

Sikh women tie their uncut hair in a bun, or plait it, and prefer to wear **kameez**, **salwar** and **duppatta**.

A Sikh place of worship is called a gurdwara. You can see the **Nishan Sahib** flying outside the gurdwara.

Sikhs have ten Gurus and their teachings are written in the Guru Granth Sahib.

Everyone takes off their shoes and covers their head before entering the prayer hall.

Everyone bows before the Guru Granth Sahib. This is to show respect to the Gurus' teachings.

In the gurdwara, everyone listens to the **shabads** from the Guru Granth Sahib, which are sung by **ragis**.

Today Jasbir Kaur is leading the service. Both men and women can lead services in the gurdwaras.

Everyone cooks together in the **langar**.

In the gurdwara, after the service, everyone eats together. This is to show that all people belong to God's big family.

These children are learning Punjabi at weekend school at the gurdwara, so that they can read the Guru Granth Sahib.

Most gurdwaras hold classes on Saturdays or Sundays to teach the **harmonium**, **tabla** and singing.

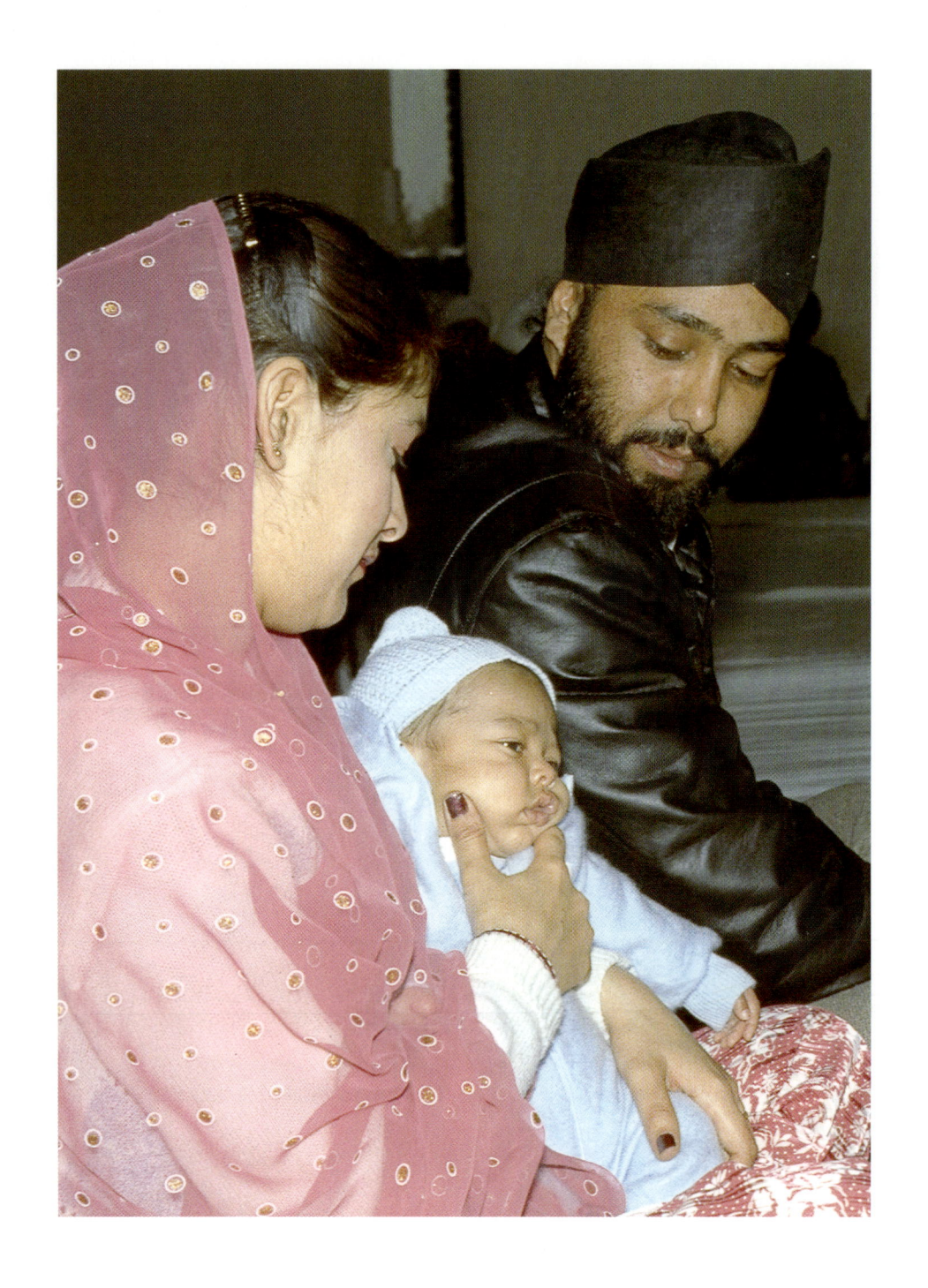

A newborn baby's first visit outside the home is to the gurdwara. The first letter of the shabad that is read will be used when naming the baby.

This couple have decided to call their daughter Raminder, as the first letter of the shabad was 'R'. Girls and boys also have second names. Girls have the second name Kaur and boys have the name Singh.

Mona and Harinder are getting married today. They are standing side by side in front of the Guru Granth Sahib, ready for the marriage ceremony to begin.

During their marriage ceremony Mona and Harinder go round the Guru Granth Sahib four times.

Sikh festivals are called gurpurabs. Today is Baisakhi gurpurab. Many hymns are sung as the Sikh flag is removed from the flag pole and replaced with a new one.

This is the Golden Temple at Amritsar. At Diwali, Sikhs remember Guru Hargobind, the sixth Guru, who arrived at the Golden Temple after helping to free 52 princes from the Emperor's jail. Diwali is celebrated with bright lights and fireworks.

Notes for Teachers

Pages 4 & 5 Sikhism was founded by Guru Nanak who was born in 1469 CE in Punjab in India. Guru Nanak established the system of Guruship and was followed by nine Gurus. Guru Gobind Singh, the tenth Guru, gave the Guruship to the Sikh holy book, the Guru Granth Sahib, and ended the line of human Gurus. The Guru Granth Sahib contains Sikh teachings written by the Gurus themselves and by Saints whose views were in accord with the Gurus.

Pages 6 & 7 Practising Sikhs do not cut their hair: keeping uncut hair is one of the symbols of the Sikh faith. Young boys tie their hair in a knot on top of their heads, which they sometimes cover with a patka (small turban) or handkerchief. Girls and women plait their hair, wear it in a bun or keep it loose. Sikhs who cut their hair are called Sehajdhari Sikhs. As well as the Sikh symbol of uncut hair (Kes) there are four other symbols of Sikhism: Kanga (comb), Kara (steel bangle), Kachera (shorts) and Kirpan (sword).

Pages 8 & 9 At a turban ceremony in the gurdwara, shabads are sung and the Sikh common prayer, the Ardas, is said asking God's blessing for the ceremony. The turban is then tied by a relative or a friend.

Pages 10 & 11 Sikh men usually wear western clothes such as trousers and jackets, but traditional clothes may be worn on special occasions or when visiting a gurdwara. Sikh women wear western clothes or Punjabi clothes. Punjabi clothes consist of a kameez (long shirt), salwar (trousers) and duppatta (long scarf).

Pages 12 & 13 Every gurdwara has the Sikh flag, the Nishan Sahib, flying outside it. In the middle of the flag is a two edged sword called the Khanda. The Khanda represents justice and freedom. Around the Khanda is a circle called a Chakra which reminds Sikhs of God's infinite power. On the outside of the Khanda are two Kirpans (swords) which remind Sikhs of their spiritual and secular responsibilities. The Guru Granth Sahib contains all the Sikh teachings written by the ten Gurus. The Sikh Gurus teach that there is one God and all humans are equal. Three important rules that Sikhs should remember are: meditate on the divine name using passages from the Guru Granth Sahib, earn one's own living, and share time, talents and earnings with others less fortunate.

Pages 14 & 15 Everyone who visits the gurdwara shows their respect by removing shoes, covering their heads and bowing before the Guru Granth Sahib.

Pages 16 & 17 The whole of the Guru Granth Sahib is written in poetry and arranged in stanzas called 'shabads'. The shabads can be sung and many gurdwaras employ professional singers called ragis. Any man or woman may read the Guru

Granth Sahib to the congregation, but often it is read by an appointed 'granthi' (a reader, who performs ceremonies and reads prayers).

Pages 18 & 19 The langar is the common kitchen or dining hall of a gurdwara. All people who attend a service at the gurdwara are expected to stay afterwards to eat together. This is a reminder that people of all colours, classes and faiths belong to the same family and therefore should be treated equally. Volunteers from the community cook and distribute the food, which is always vegetarian, so that everyone is able to eat.

Pages 20 & 21 Many children attend Saturday and Sunday classes held in the gurdwaras to learn Punjabi and to play musical instruments.

Pages 22 & 23 The birth of a baby is celebrated at the naming ceremony in the gurdwara or the home. The ceremony is performed in the presence of the Guru Granth Sahib. At the end of the service, the Guru Granth Sahib is opened for the hukam (a random reading for guidance). The family listens for the first letter of the first word of the shabad that is read and chooses a name for the child that begins with that letter. To give women the same equality as men, Guru Gobind Singh gave women the name Kaur (princess) and gave men the name Singh (lion).

Pages 24 & 25 Sikh marriage is not only a social contract between two equal partners but also a spiritual union in which partners support and enrich each other's lives. Four special shabads are read and sung, and after each one the couple rise and walk around the Guru Granth Sahib.

Pages 26 & 27 Sikh festivals such as Baisakhi are celebrated in gurdwaras throughout the world. Baisakhi day usually falls in April. It was at this festival that Guru Gobind Singh conducted the first Amrit ceremony. Amrit is the initiation ceremony into the Sikh community. Traditionally on this day, the Nishan Sahib, the Sikh flag, is renewed. A service led by five Sikhs in traditional dress is held in the gurdwara. The flag post is taken down and the flag cloth removed. The flag post is washed, and a new flag cloth attached and rehoisted. Also on Baisakhi the Amrit ceremony is performed and there are competitions in sports, martial arts and music. Diwali celebrates Guru Hargobind's arrival at the Golden Temple at Amritsar in India. The Guru was imprisoned by the Emperor for not accepting Islam. The Emperor realised that the Guru was a holy man and felt ashamed of what he had done. He ordered his release. But the Guru refused to go unless fifty-two other Hindu princes were also released. The Emperor agreed that those princes who could hold on to the Guru's cloak while he went through a narrow gate would be freed. The Guru wore a cloak with fifty-two tassels and the princes held on to them and were freed.

Glossary

duppatta A long scarf.

gurdwara A building in which Sikhs meet together and worship.

Guru Granth Sahib An important book for all Sikhs.

harmonium An Indian musical instrument with a keyboard.

kameez A long shirt.

langar The gurdwara dining room where Sikhs cook and eat together.

Nishan Sahib The Sikh flag.

patka A head covering worn by Sikh boys.

ragis Sikh musicians who read and sing shabads from the Guru Granth Sahib.

salwar Trousers.

shabads Hymns from the Guru Granth Sahib.

tabla Indian drums.

Further Information

Books to Read

A Year of Religious Festivals: My Sikh Year by Cath Senker (Hodder Wayland, 2005)

Celebrations!: Baisakhi by Mandy Ross (Heinemann, 2002)

Holy Places: The Golden Temple by Victoria Parker (Heinemann, 2003)

Our Culture: Sikh by Jenny Wood (Franklin Watts, 2003)

Places of Worship: Sikh Gurdwaras by Gopinder Kaur Panesa (Heinemann, 1999)

Talking About My Faith: I am Sikh by Cath Senker (Franklin Watts, 2005)

The Facts About Sikhism by Alison Cooper (Hodder Wayland, 2004)

Useful Organisations

Sikh Educational and Cultural Association (UK)
Sat Nam Cottage
3 Compton Gardens, Kinver,
Dudley,
West Midlands,
DY7 6DS

Sikh Foundation
580 College Avenue,
Palo Alto,
CA 94306
USA
www.sikhfoundation.org

Sikhism for Children
http://atschool.eduweb.co.uk/carolrb/sikhism/sikhism1.html

The Sikhism Home Page
www.sikhs.org

The website addresses (URLs) included in this book were valid at the time of going to press. However, because of the nature of the Internet, it is possible that some addresses may have changed, or sites may have changed or closed down since publication. While the authors and publisher regret any inconvenience this may cause readers, no responsibility for any such changes can be accepted by either the authors or the publisher.

Index

babies 22, 23
Baisakhi 26
beards 10

clothes 6, 10, 11, 14

Diwali 27
duppatta 11, 30

family 4, 19
festivals 26, 27
flags 12, 26
food 18, 19

Golden Temple 27
gurdwara 9, 12, 16, 17, 19, 21, 22, 30

gurpurabs 26
Guru Granth Sahib 5, 13, 15, 16, 20, 24, 25, 30
Guru Hargobind 27

hair 6, 7, 11

kameez 11, 30

langar 18, 30

marriage 24, 25

names 22, 23
Nishan Sahib 12, 30

patka 6, 30
Punjabi 20

ragis 16, 30

salwar 11, 30
school 20, 21
shabads 16, 22, 23, 30

teachings 13, 15
turbans 6, 8, 9, 10

worship 12–19